Mr Drummond was

his ears.

People say Mary Maloney is a good runner – for a *girl.* Of course, she will never beat the fastest boy. Boys are stronger than girls. They'll always run faster. It's a scientific fact. That's what her teachers tell her. But people thought the world was flat, once, didn't they?

Mary doesn't believe what everyone says. She *knows* she can win against the boys. But *showing* that she can is not so easy – not when so many people want to stop her trying . . .

Jeremy Taylor was born in Bristol, England, in 1962. He studied at London University and taught in a school in London for a year. He began writing after he left England in 1987 and went to Mannheim, Germany: he wrote his first book with the help of a girl he met in a pub . . . Since then he has written nineteen more books and sixty-nine short stories.

He now lives in the Czech Republic. At one time he worked as a teacher there 'just to keep out of trouble.' But now he spends most of his time writing. He also likes cycling and swimming. In 1983, he cycled alone to the north of Norway.

OTHER TITLES IN THE SERIES

Level 1
Girl Meets Boy
The Hen and the Bull
The Medal of Brigadier Gerard

Level 2
The Birds
Chocky
Don't Look Now
Emily
The Fox
The Ghost of Genny Castle
Grandad's Eleven
The Lady in the Lake
Money to Burn
Persuasion
The Railway Children
The Room in the Tower and Other Ghost Stories
Simply Suspense
Treasure Island
Under the Greenwood Tree

Level 3
Black Beauty
The Black Cat and Other Stories
The Book of Heroic Failures
A Catskill Eagle
The Darling Buds of May
Dubliners
Earthdark
Jane Eyre
King Solomon's Mines
Madame Doubtfire
The Man with Two Shadows and Other Ghost Stories
More Heroic Failures
Mrs Dalloway
My Family and Other Animals
Rain Man
The Reluctant Queen
Sherlock Holmes and the Mystery of Boscombe Pool
The Thirty-nine Steps
Time Bird
Twice Shy

Level 4
The Boys from Brazil
The Breathing Method
The Danger
Detective Work
The Doll's House and Other Stories
Dracula
Far from the Madding Crowd
Farewell, My Lovely
Glitz
Gone with the Wind, Part 1
Gone with the Wind, Part 2
The House of Stairs
The Locked Room and Other Horror Stories
The Mill on the Floss
The Mosquito Coast
The Picture of Dorian Gray
Strangers on a Train
White Fang

Level 5
The Baby Party and Other Stories
The Body
The Firm
The Grass is Singing
Jude the Obscure
The Old Jest
The Pelican Brief
Pride and Prejudice
Prime Suspect
A Twist in the Tale
The Warden
Web

Level 6
The Edge
The Long Goodbye
Misery
Mrs Packletide's Tiger and Other Stories
The Moonstone
Presumed Innocent
A Tale of Two Cities
The Thorn Birds
Wuthering Heights

Channel Runner

JEREMY TAYLOR

Level 3

Series Editor: Derek Strange

PENGUIN BOOKS

PENGUIN BOOKS

Published by the Penguin Group
Penguin Books Ltd, 27 Wrights Lane, London W8 5TZ, England
Penguin Books USA Inc., 375 Hudson Street, New York, New York 10014, USA
Penguin Books Australia Ltd, Ringwood, Victoria, Australia
Penguin Books Canada Ltd, 10 Alcorn Avenue, Toronto, Ontario, Canada M4V 3B2
Penguin Books (NZ) Ltd, 182–190 Wairau Road, Auckland 10, New Zealand

Penguin Books Ltd, Registered Offices: Harmondsworth, Middlesex, England

First published by Penguin Books 1995
1 3 5 7 9 10 8 6 4 2

Illustrations by Rowan Clifford

Typeset by Datix International Limited, Bungay, Suffolk
Printed in England by Clays Ltd, St Ives plc
Set in 11/14 pt Monophoto Bembo

To the teacher:

In addition to all the language forms of Levels One and Two, which are used again at this level of the series, the main verb forms and tenses used at Level Three are:

- past continuous verbs, present perfect simple verbs, conditional clauses (using the 'first' or 'open future' conditional), question tags and further common phrasal verbs
- modal verbs: *have (got) to and don't have to* (to express obligation), *need to* and *needn't* (to express necessity), *could* and *was able to* (to describe past ability), *could* and *would* (in offers and polite requests for help), and *shall* (for future plans, offers and suggestions).

Also used are:

- relative pronouns: *who*, *that* and *which* (in defining clauses)
- conjunctions: *if* and *since* (for time or reason), *so that* (for purpose or result) and *while*
- indirect speech (questions)
- participle clauses.

Specific attention is paid to vocabulary development in the Vocabulary Work exercises at the end of the book. These exercises are aimed at training students to enlarge their vocabulary systematically through intelligent reading and effective use of a dictionary.

To the student:

Dictionary Words:

- When you read this book, you will find that some words are darker black than the others on the page. Look them up in your dictionary, if you do not already know them, or try to guess the meaning of the words first, without a dictionary.

CHAPTER ONE

'OK, I'll see you all on Monday. Have a good weekend and don't forget to answer the questions on page seventy-three!'

It was the end of Mr Hunt's **science** lesson and the end of the day. The class of fourteen-year-olds left the room quickly to get outside into the sunshine. Mr Hunt was looking at some papers when he heard someone at his desk.

'Mr Hunt, can I ask you a question?' Mary Maloney stood in front of him.

'Of course, Mary. What is it?'

'Do you think men are better than women?'

Mr Hunt stopped reading and thought about Mary's question. 'Well, what do you mean by "better"? I'm a scientist and I know that it's a scientific **fact** that men are stronger than women and can run faster than women. Men have stronger arms and legs than women.'

'What about intelligence? Do you think men are more intelligent than women?'

'Again, intelligence is a very difficult thing to count, but most of the world's great scientists have been men. I don't know if it is because men are more intelligent. Why do you ask, Mary?'

'I don't think it's true.'

'What don't you think is true?'

'That men are, in any way, better than women.'

'But Mary, these are scientific facts. In all sports, women cannot run as fast as men. They cannot jump as high as men and they cannot throw things as far as men.'

'Just because women *haven't* run as fast or jumped as high as men, does it mean that they *can't*?'

'But Mary, these are scientific facts. In all sports, women cannot run as fast as men. They cannot jump as high as men and they cannot throw things as far as men.'

'No, Mary, it doesn't mean that, but . . .' Mr Hunt smiled at Mary. He liked her. She was a good student who worked hard. 'Look Mary, everyone can only do their best, men and women. I don't think it is important *who* is better. As long as everyone does their best.'

Mary smiled at Mr Hunt. 'I'll have some more questions for you next week.'

'That's all right with me, Mary. I'll do my best to answer any of your questions.'

Mary Maloney walked out of the room and Mr Hunt watched her. He thought about what she said. Did she really think that scientific facts about men and women were wrong? Mr Hunt shook his head. Then he picked up his papers, turned off the lights and then he, too, went out into the early spring sunshine.

CHAPTER TWO

'OK Mary, that's eight kilometres.'

Mary was hot. Her legs felt tired. But something inside her told her to go on running.

'Where's she going?' Darren Green, the sports teacher watched Mary. She continued round the **track** for the twenty-first time.

'Australia?' said Peter Morris, who was standing next to Darren. 'Do you think she's going to win the **race** on Saturday?'

'Of course she will,' said Darren. 'There are only three schools in the race. There's no one as good as Mary in any of them.'

Darren Green looked at his watch. He shook his head slowly and watched Mary Maloney running round the track. After eight and a half kilometres she still looked fresh.

'She's not bad, is she? – for a girl.' It was James Curtis, the school's best ten-thousand-metre runner. Well, James thought he was the school's best ten-thousand-metre runner.

Peter and Darren both looked at him. 'She's not bad, for a girl or a boy,' said Peter, still watching Mary.

James looked at him and smiled. 'Are you in love with her or something?'

'No, I just think she's a great runner.'

James smiled again and shook his head.

After ten kilometres, Mary finally stopped running.

'That was great, Mary. How are you feeling?' asked Darren.

'Fine,' said Mary.

'You'll have no problems on Saturday, Mary. You're a great runner.'

'Do you think so?'

'Sure I do. There probably isn't a girl in this country as good as you.'

Mary looked up at Darren. 'What about the boys?'

'What *about* the boys?'

'Am I good enough to **beat** the boys?'

'You mean a race between you and the boys?'

'That's right,' said Mary.

'Well, I'm sure you could beat some of them.'

'Only some?'

'Come on, Mary, are you **crazy**? You're a girl. You're a great runner but you can't beat the boys. Men are stronger than women and can run faster than women. Men have stronger arms and legs than women.'

'I've heard that already today,' said Mary. 'Do you think it's true?'

'Well, yes. It's a scientific fact. There's nothing we can do to change it.'

'She's not bad, is she? – for a girl.'

'People once thought the Earth was **flat**. They thought that was a scientific fact.'

'But, Mary, that was a long time ago. We're talking about modern scientific facts.'

'Does that mean that all modern scientific facts are right and none of them are wrong?'

'Well, perhaps . . .' Darren Green could now see what was in Mary's head. He now knew why she ran ten kilometres round the track instead of only eight.

'What do you want to do?' he asked.

'Well, it's too late to start in the race on Saturday. How about the **trials** next week?'

'I'm sorry, Mary, I'm still not sure what you want.'

'I want to race against the boys.'

'Did you hear that?' said James Curtis. 'She wants to run against boys! I knew it, the girl is crazy!'

Peter looked at James. 'Are you worried?'

'Me? No way. No girl will ever beat me.'

'Well?' Mary looked at Darren.

'I . . . I . . . don't know. I don't know what the **committee** will say.'

'I do,' said Mary and she stood up. 'They'll say no. They're just a group of stupid old men who aren't interested in changing anything.'

'I'll do what I can, Mary, but I can't promise you anything.'

After her run, Mary took a cold shower. She always enjoyed feeling the cold water on her shoulders. The other runners thought she was crazy. Perhaps I am, she often thought.

CHAPTER THREE

On her way home, Mary went into the library.

'Hello, Mary, how are things?'

'Hi, Mrs Huett, not so bad.'

'Have you won any races this year?'

'A few,' Mary smiled.

'I've got a book which I think you'll like.' Mrs Huett brought out a book from under her desk.

'Penny Dean,' read Mary. 'She's a swimmer, isn't she?'

'That's right, but I think she's a little more special than that.'

'More special?'

'Read the book and find out.'

'I'll bring it back tomorrow.'

'Bye, Mary.'

♦

That evening, after a quick supper, Mary ran over to her friend Hannah's house. They had to learn about North African countries for a lesson the next day and they planned to study together. They went up to Hannah's room. Mary lay on the floor, then Hannah sat on her knees.

'I'm ready when you are, Mary.'

'I'm ready.' Mary put her hands behind her head and lifted her head and shoulders off the ground.

'Question one. What's the longest river in Africa?' asked Hannah.

'The Nile,' answered Mary before lying flat on the floor again. She lifted herself up for the second time.

'Question two. Which country is between Sudan and Nigeria?'

'Umm, Chad?'

'Good, down you go.' Mary rested while Hannah found another question. In thirty-eight questions, Mary got thirty-six questions right.

'OK, question number thirty-nine. Which North African country has got the most oil?'

'Libya?'

'Right again.' Mary went down slowly.

'Question number forty. A man swims along the coast from Rabat in Morocco to Israel. How many North African countries does he visit?'

Mary held her head and shoulders up while she counted. 'Four and three quarters.' She started to go down again.

'Wait a minute, Mary. How can it be four and three quarters?'

Mary held her head a few centimetres from the floor, 'Morocco, Algeria, Tunisia, Libya and three quarters of Egypt.'

'What do you mean, three quarters?'

'Sinai is part of Egypt but it's Asia, not Africa.'

'It isn't.'

'It is.'

'It . . . Are you sure?'

'Yes.'

'OK, down you go.'

Mary lay on the floor, her tongue out like a dog on a hot beach. Hannah took off her pullover and lay on the floor. 'OK, now me, but I can only do twenty-five questions. I'm not as strong as you.'

Hannah only got one wrong out of the first twenty-four questions. Slowly, she came up for question number twenty-five.

'Who swam the English Channel in the fastest time ever?' asked Mary excitedly.

Mary held her head a few centimetres from the floor, 'Morocco, Algeria, Tunisia, Libya and three quarters of Egypt.'

'That's not about North Africa!'

'I know, but the answer is very interesting.' Mary had a big smile on her face.

'Um, I don't know any Channel swimmers. I don't know, what's his name?'

Mary shook her head and sat with her back against Hannah's bed.

'What's wrong?'

'Your answer.'

'But I didn't give you an answer. I said "I don't know".'

'You said, "What's his name?"'

'And?'

'You thought it was a man.'

'And?'

'It wasn't. It was a woman called Penny Dean.'

'A woman swam faster than a man? But that's impossible!'

'Oh no, it isn't,' said Mary.

♦

In bed that night, Mary finished the book about Penny Dean that Mrs Huett gave her. While she went to sleep she thought about her running. What Penny Dean did in the water, she would do on the race track. She would be the Channel Runner.

CHAPTER FOUR

Alistair Hunt often went to school by bike. Most of the other teachers either drove or took the bus. He liked to get into school early to do some work before all the students arrived.

'Morning, **sir**!' Mary Maloney *always* went to school by bike.

'Good morning, Mary. How are you?'

'Feeling great. Do you want a race?'

'Not this morning, Mary.'

'Does the name Penny Dean mean anything to you?'

'I can't say it does. Is she a pop singer?'

'She's the greatest Channel swimmer of all time, man or woman.'

'I didn't know that.'

'You do now,' said Mary. 'She's the Channel Swimmer and I'm the Channel Runner. See you later!'

♦

'So I think that's all for today, so I . . . are you all right, Mr Green?'

'Yes, I'm fine, but there's one more thing I'd like to say.'

'And that is?'

'I think some of you have seen one of my runners, a girl called Mary Maloney.'

'What about her?' The **chairman** did not hide the fact that he wanted to end the **meeting** and go home.

'Well, she's a great runner and I think . . .'

'Tell us what you want to say, Mr Green.'

'She wants to race against the boys at the trials next week.'

The **members** of the committee suddenly woke up.

'She wants to do what?'

'She's tired of winning all her races against girls. She believes that women are as good as men at sports. She wants to . . .'

'How stupid!'

'The girl needs a good doctor.'

'And Mr Green,' said the Chairman. 'Do you **support** Miss Maloney's ideas?'

'I told her that I would ask the committee.'

'Mr Green, I have never heard anything so stupid in all my life!'

'You haven't answered my question, Mr Green. Do you, or do you not, support Miss Maloney?'

'Well . . . I . . . I'm not sure . . . Well, yes, I think I do.'

Chairman Drummond stood up. He looked down at Darren Green and shook his head slowly. 'Mr Green, I have never heard anything so stupid in all my **life**! Meeting closed.'

CHAPTER FIVE

'OK, we're going to do an eight-kilometre run tonight. Is everybody ready?' asked James Curtis.

Everybody was ready.

'OK, let's go!'

A group of eighteen boys left the changing rooms and ran across the school playing fields. It was quite a cold evening and the runners wore warm clothes. Some of them wore hats.

James Curtis looked round at his runners. Some of the younger boys were finding it difficult. Others could run fifteen kilometres without any problems. He would speak to Darren Green about who they should choose for the trials next week. Early on the run, Mark Hudson fell down and hurt his foot. He wouldn't be ready for the trials.

After four kilometres, James Curtis stopped running. The boys ran past him and he counted the heads. He wanted to see that the group was together. He counted the heads quickly. Seventeen? And himself. That was eighteen. Surely Mark Hudson wasn't with them again? James ran after the group.

'Where's Mark Hudson?'

'He went back,' answered one of the runners. 'He hurt his foot. You saw him.'

James Curtis shook his head and the boys ran on along the river.

'Last kilometre coming up!' called James.

It was not a real race, but in the last kilometre many of the runners tried to run as fast as James. With only four hundred metres to go, there was only one runner next to him. He looked to see who it was but the runner was wearing a hat. 'Do you want to race?' asked James.

The runner with the hat said nothing. Suddenly, the mystery runner disappeared up the road.

'Hey! Where are you going?'

James did not get an answer. He stood and watched the runner in the black shirt with the letters 'CR' on the back.

CHAPTER SIX

'Mrs Maloney?'

'That's right.'

'My name's Darren Green. I'm Mary's sports teacher. Is Mary in?'

'She's gone out for a run but I think she'll be back soon. Would you like to come in and wait?'

'If that's OK.'

Over coffee and a piece of cake Darren told Mrs Maloney about the committee meeting.

'So there's not a lot she can do. She told me about her plans. Did she tell you about Penny Dean?' asked Mrs Maloney.

'No, I haven't seen her for a few days.'

'So you don't know about the Channel Runner?'

'No. What is it?' asked Darren.

'It's Mary. She read a book about Penny Dean,' said Mrs Maloney.

Suddenly, the mystery runner disappeared up the road.

'Who's Penny Dean?'

'She's the fastest Channel swimmer of all time, man or woman. Mary says that if Penny Dean is the Channel Swimmer, then she'll be the Channel Runner.'

Darren Green shook his head. 'She's a great girl.'

'Who is?'

Darren Green and Mrs Maloney looked up to see Mary in her black shirt with 'CR' on the back. 'You are,' said her mother.

Mary smiled at Darren. 'They said no, didn't they?'

'I tried but . . .'

'Don't worry,' said Mary. 'Thanks for trying.'

'I don't know what we can do now.'

'Well, I've got one or two little plans.' Mary smiled a mysterious smile.

'I'll see you at the race on Saturday, Channel Runner,' said Darren, standing up.

'I'll be there,' said Mary.

CHAPTER SEVEN

'I say, Hodgkins, what's the first race?'

Mr Hodgkins looked at the programme. 'It's the boys' ten thousand metres.'

'Very good,' said Mr Drummond, the chairman of the sports committee. Also in the sports **stadium** there were a lot of happy parents. Many of them were sure that their children would soon win Olympic gold.

'Here come the boys now,' said Mr Hodgkins.

James Curtis and about thirty other boys were standing on the track near the starting line. A minute later the boys from the three schools were running along the track and out of the stadium on their ten-thousand-metre run.

'Well, I've got one or two little plans.' Mary smiled a mysterious smile.

It was a warm day and in the corner of the stadium an ice-cream seller was doing good business. After about forty-five minutes, the first of the ten-thousand-metre runners came back into the sports stadium. James Curtis was in a group of six runners. With four hundred metres to go, James moved away from the group and won the race by five metres.

◆

Downstairs in the changing rooms the girls were getting ready for their ten-thousand-metre run.

'Mary, what is *that*?'

'What do you think it is?'

'I can see what it is,' answered Hannah, 'but you're not going to race in it . . .' She stopped. Seeing the look on Mary's face, she asked, 'Are you?'

'Do you think they'll notice me?' asked Mary.

'Something tells me they will,' Hannah laughed.

Minutes later the girls came out of the changing rooms and went towards the starting line.

'Hodgkins?'

'Yes, Mr Drummond?'

'Is this the race that that girl is running in?'

'Do you mean Mary Maloney?'

'Yes, that's the one.'

'Yes, sir, she'll be number twenty-two.'

'Mmm, I'll look out for her.'

The girls got ready for the race and Mr Drummond looked for runner number twenty-two. Suddenly he jumped to his feet.

'*Hodgkins*!' Chairman Drummond was red in the face.

'Yes, sir? Are you all right, sir?'

'No, I'm not all right, Hodgkins!' Chairman Drummond's face was now the colour of a tomato. 'What is *that*?'

Mr Hodgkins looked where Mr Drummond was pointing. 'It looks like a **chimpanzee**, sir – or someone dressed like a chimpanzee.'

Mr Drummond and Mr Hodgkins watched as runner number twenty-two, dressed like a chimpanzee, ran to the starting line.

Suddenly the group of thirty-five girls were on their way. Runner number twenty-two ran past her friends and waved at them. Darren Green shook his head. He also found it very hard not to smile.

'Are you all right, sir?'

Mr Drummond did not speak until the last girl left the stadium. Before he spoke he put his hand into the pocket of his jacket and pulled out a small bottle. He took a quick drink and put the bottle back into his jacket pocket. 'She's crazy, I'm sure the poor girl is crazy.' Mr Drummond looked at Mr Hodgkins. 'I hope you don't find this amusing, Hodgkins?'

'No, no, sir. It's very serious,' replied Mr Hodgkins, trying his best not to laugh.

Mr Drummond could not watch the other sports. When he tried to watch a high jumper or a long jumper, he could only see a stupid chimpanzee waving at the crowd of people in the stadium.

Suddenly, he saw the chimpanzee again, only this time it was real. The chimpanzee waved again as she came into the stadium. She ran round the track to the finishing line. She was in the last hundred metres when the second runner came into the stadium.

The chimpanzee got nearer the line. Then she slowed down and sat down just in front of the line. From somewhere she brought out a small banana and started to eat it.

Almost everyone in the stadium was laughing. Only the small group of men round Mr Drummond were not laughing.

From somewhere she brought out a small banana and started to eat it.

Mr Drummond was very, very angry. Smoke was coming out of his ears.

The second runner got near the line and the chimpanzee put the back of her hands on the floor. She moved round and made noises just like a real chimpanzee.

But then, just before the other girl reached her, the chimpanzee put her head over the line and won the race.

CHAPTER EIGHT

After the races, there was a special committee meeting. The twelve members of the committee sat round the table. At one end of the table sat Chairman Drummond, at the sides were the other eleven committee members and a very uncomfortable Darren Green. He knew why there was a meeting and he knew how angry Mr Drummond was.

A few minutes before seven there was a knock at the door.

'Come in!'

'Evening all!'

Darren held his head in his hands.

'Sit down, Miss Maloney!'

'Thank you.' Mary smiled at the members of the committee.

'Right, Miss Maloney, I want an explanation.'

'An explanation, Mr Drummond?'

'You know perfectly well what I'm talking about!'

'Oh, you mean the race today? Oh right. Well, I stayed with the best runners for the first part of the race, but with about two thousand metres to go I . . .'

'*Miss Maloney*!'

'Yes, Mr Drummond?'

'You dressed like a stupid chimpanzee for the race today. We would like an explanation.'

'Three things: number one, I don't think chimpanzees are stupid. Number two, I won the race today, which you are surely happy about. Number three, what I did was a **protest**.'

'A protest?' said Mr Drummond. 'Would you like to tell us what you are protesting against? Chimpanzees in **zoos**, perhaps?'

Some of the committee members laughed at Chairman Drummond's words.

'It's true I'm not happy about chimpanzees in zoos, but this protest was about something this committee decided last week. I think that women are just as good as men in every way. There are some important trials next week. I want to race against the boys. You say that I can't and that's why I'm protesting.'

Mr Drummond looked at the other members of the committee before speaking. 'Miss Maloney, I know that you are young and that you have some strange ideas. But as long as I am chairman of this committee, no girl will run against boys. Do you understand me?'

'Yes and no.'

'What do you mean, "yes and no"?'

'I understand what you say but I don't understand why you say it.'

Chairman Drummond was very, very angry. 'Miss Maloney, leave this room immediately!'

'OK,' said Mary. 'I'm on my way. It was nice talking to you.'

CHAPTER NINE

'They called me almost as soon as I got home. They said I can't run for three months.' Mary was with Peter and Hannah at the local sports centre.

'But they can't do that. You didn't break any rules,' said Hannah.

'I asked Darren about it. They *can* stop me from running if they want to,' said Mary.

'But we must try to stop them,' said Peter.

'Do you think I won't try to stop them?' replied Mary. 'Hannah's brother works for the Waterbridge Observer newspaper. He took some photos of the chimpanzee winning the ten-thousand-metres race yesterday. He says they're wonderful pictures but he needs a good story to go with them. I think I've got a story for him.'

Peter said nothing. Mary and Hannah looked at him.

'Peter, are you OK?' asked Hannah.

'I'm fine. I'm thinking.'

He got up and walked out quickly.

'Where's he going?'

'No idea.'

Peter was on his way to the telephone. He had a plan. It would not be easy but he wanted to help the Channel Runner.

'Can I speak to James Curtis please? . . . Hi James, this is Peter . . . Listen, I'm calling about Mary, the Channel Runner, . . . No, she's not my girlfriend . . . The committee says she can't run for three months . . . Yes, just for her protest as a chimpanzee . . . Well, I thought we can say we won't run in the trials if Mary can't run against boys . . . I know . . . Yes, I know, James, . . . I run every day as well but . . . James? Hello? Oh no.'

CHAPTER TEN

On Monday afternoon, the older boys met in the sports **hall**. Peter did not want to speak to James. When most of the boys were ready, James shouted for quiet. The boys knew why and were quickly silent.

'I have in my hand a piece of paper,' said James. 'A very important piece of paper. Here are the names of the boys who will run in the trials on Thursday. The fastest runners in the races on Thursday will find themselves in races against the best runners in the country. But, before I read the list there is another important question that we have to answer. Peter Morris has got something to ask you.'

Peter suddenly found about seventy pairs of eyes looking at him. 'It's about Mary Maloney,' began Peter.

'Is that the girl they call the Channel Runner?' asked one of the high jumpers.

'Yes, that's her. She wants to race against boys. The sports committee think she's crazy and they say she can't. That's why she dressed like a chimpanzee on Saturday, to protest. Now they say that she can't run for three months.'

'What do you want us to do about it?' asked James.

'Well, you've got the list of names for the trials from this school, right?'

'That's right,' said James.

'And you're going to give that list to the committee tonight, right?'

'Right again.'

'I want us to put Mary Maloney's name on the list. We can tell the committee that if Mary can't run against boys, we'll **boycott** the trials.'

Suddenly there was a lot of noise. Some of the boys

'I want us to put Mary Maloney's name on the list. We can tell the committee that if Mary can't run against boys, we'll boycott *the trials.'*

shouted angrily at Peter, while other boys, who knew Mary, wanted to support her.

'OK, OK,' shouted James. 'I know what to do. If you want me to put Mary Maloney's name on this list, put your hand up.'

Peter and James both counted the hands. There were thirty-five.

'And who *doesn't* want me to put Mary Maloney's name on the list?' asked James, putting up his own hand.

This time only thirty-three hands went up.

'Looks like you've done it, Morris,' said James, and he wrote Mary Maloney's name on the list of runners to run in the ten-thousand-metre trials.

'Thanks a lot,' said Peter to the other sportsmen.

CHAPTER ELEVEN

'Come in!'

James Curtis went in.

'Ah, James, have you got the list with you?'

James gave the list to Chairman Drummond.

'Good, good. This . . .' Suddenly Mr Drummond's mouth fell open. He looked up at James. 'Are you trying to be funny, Curtis?'

'No, sir, I didn't want to, but . . .'

'Mr Curtis, did you write Mary Maloney's name on this list?'

'Well, yes, sir, but . . .'

'But what?'

'I think there's something I must tell you.'

'And that is?'

James felt very uncomfortable. 'The boys won't run in the trials on Thursday if Mary Maloney cannot run against us.'

'*Won't run*?! But that's crazy! There is nothing, I repeat nothing, that will change this rule. Mary Maloney cannot run against boys. Do you understand me, Curtis?'

'Yes, sir.'

♦

'So how was the meeting?' asked Peter.

'Bad, very bad,' said James. 'I told them I didn't want Mary to run against the boys, but they didn't listen to me. Now I'm not so sure. If she wants to run against boys, why not? I still don't think she can win.'

'But you think she can try?'

James Curtis thought for a few seconds. 'Yeah, why not?'

CHAPTER TWELVE

At breakfast the next day, Chairman Drummond was eating a plate of eggs and sausages. Mrs Drummond gave him a cup of tea and the newspaper. Suddenly Mrs Drummond heard an angry shout behind her and she dropped a bottle of milk on the floor.

'*Brenda*!'

'What is it, Alfred?'

'Look at this!'

Chairman Drummond showed the front page to his wife. There was a large photograph of the race track with runner number twenty-two holding a banana in her hand. Mrs Drummond sat next to her husband and they both read the story. Mrs Drummond thought that she saw smoke coming out of her husband's ears again.

Chairman and Mrs Drummond were not the only people

'What are you going to do now, Chairman Drummond?'

to read the story. Many people read about the girl, the Channel Runner. They also read about the committee's rules against girls racing with boys, and the boycott that the boys were planning, not only in Mary's school, but also in many other schools.

The story started with the question, 'What are you going to do now, Chairman Drummond?'

CHAPTER THIRTEEN

It was quite a surprise for James Curtis to get a kiss from Mary Maloney.

'What was that for?'

'For calling the boys in the other schools.'

'Well, Mary if you want to run against boys then I'm not going to stop you.'

'Mary!' It was Peter with Darren Green.

Mary waved at them. They ran over to Mary and ran next to her round the track.

'Hi, how are things?'

'Fine, thanks,' said Darren. 'Listen, Mary, I've heard there's going to be a special committee meeting tomorrow at twelve o'clock. First, there'll be a closed meeting but then there'll be another meeting for everybody. I've heard that the TV people will be there.'

'That will be interesting.'

'You've made quite a few problems for a number of people, Mary.'

'You can't make an omelette without breaking eggs,' said the Channel Runner. 'Oh, Peter, thanks very much for talking to the boys in the sports hall. I'm sure it wasn't easy.'

Peter felt Mary's soft lips on his nose before she ran away.

♦

Peter felt Mary's soft lips on his nose before she ran away.

Later that evening, Mary had a phone call.

'Hello. Is that Mary Maloney?'

'It is. What can I do for you?'

'My name is Brenda Drummond . . .'

♦

'Morning, sir!' The Channel Runner was again on her bike next to Mr Hunt.

'Good morning, Mary. How are you this morning?'

'I'm fine, thanks. Oh, sir, do you think the world is flat?'

'No, I don't.'

'Do you think that men are better than women in any way?'

'I'll think about that one.'

'OK, sir, but don't forget about Penny Dean while you're thinking.'

'All right, Mary, I won't forget her,' he laughed.

CHAPTER FOURTEEN

All morning, most of the school was talking about the Channel Runner and the meeting at twelve o'clock. Luckily, the committee's meeting room was not far from school and just after twelve, a large number of students went there to support Mary.

'Good afternoon, this is Nicole Allen of Sunny Television reporting from Greenbrook sports stadium. Behind this door a very important meeting is going on. The meeting will decide what to do about a very special person. That special person is Mary Maloney, the Channel Runner, and she's here with me now. Mary, I see you've brought a few friends with you today.'

'Well, I don't know all of them, but I'm very happy that they're here to support me.'

'What do you think the committee will say at the end of their meeting?'

'I'm not sure, but I feel lucky today.'

'Thank you very much, Mary Channel Runner Maloney.'

Five minutes later, the door of the meeting room opened. Chairman Drummond stood in the bright sun. 'We have just had a very interesting meeting. We will hold an open meeting in the sports hall in five minutes time. Thank you.'

CHAPTER FIFTEEN

Three minutes later the sports hall was full of people: Hannah's brother and some other reporters, the television people, some teachers and many of Mary's friends were there.

A door at the side of the hall opened and the twelve members of the committee walked in. Chairman Drummond sat in the middle, the other members sat on his left and right. When Chairman Drummond stood up, the crowd became quiet.

'I would like to thank you all for coming here today. I am not a young man. I have seen many things in my life. I think there are few things that can surprise me. But in this last week I have had some very unpleasant surprises.'

The hall was silent; everyone listened to Chairman Drummond. Mary sat at the front; on her left was Peter Morris, on her right was James Curtis.

The Chairman continued. 'My first surprise was when I heard that a girl called Mary Maloney wanted to run against boys. My second surprise came when Darren Green told me that he supported Mary!'

Many people turned to look at Darren Green standing at

'What do you think the committee will say at the end of their meeting?'

the back of the hall. He looked straight at Chairman Drummond.

'Then, a great sportsman, one of the best that this town has seen for a long time, also turned against me. I can see him now sitting at the front. James Curtis, you don't know what you're doing.'

'He's going to stop *me* from running,' said James to Mary quietly.

'I'm sure there were others. I hear that another of the boys helped Mary Maloney. I don't know who it was but it was another knife in my back. I think perhaps some of the members of my own committee support Mary. But the deepest cut came yesterday. My wife Brenda has told me that I'm wrong and that Miss Mary Maloney must be free to run against boys.'

Some people smiled at Mary. Chairman Drummond continued. 'I have spoken with the committee and we have decided to choose a new Chairman. The new Chairman is to be . . . Chairwoman Brenda Drummond.'

Chairman Drummond picked up his papers and left the sports hall. Chairwoman Drummond came in and took her husband's place.

'Well, this *is* a surprise,' she said. 'I feel I am very lucky to be here today and to be your new Chairwoman. But I am only here because of one person, Miss Mary Channel Runner Maloney. Like many of you, I read about Mary Maloney in the newspaper. After I read the story I talked to my husband. We talked for a long, long time. It was not easy for me to talk to him about Mary. But I wanted to do the best I could for the Channel Runner and, you can see, it worked. I have spoken with the committee and we have decided that Mary Maloney, and any other girl, can run against boys in the ten-thousand-metres today.'

♦

Peter Morris and James Curtis lifted Mary on to their shoulders and carried her out of the sports hall.

Peter Morris and James Curtis lifted Mary on to their shoulders and carried her out of the sports hall. Round her were her friends, supporters, reporters and a Sunny TV cameraman.

CHAPTER SIXTEEN

The stadium was full and there were many people round the outside of the track. The lights were on and the crowd was waiting to see some good races. The Sunny TV cameraman, Nicole Allen and Hannah's brother were there. Of course there was only one race the reporters and TV people were really interested in. The one that started at twenty past six, the ten thousand metres.

At six fifteen the runners came out of the changing rooms. Runner number twenty-two was not as hairy as in her last race. While she got ready for the race she thought of Penny Dean. You are the Channel Swimmer and I am the Channel Runner she thought to herself. She smiled at the TV camera and waved to her friends in the stadium.

At nineteen minutes past six she went to the starting line together with twenty-four boys. The Channel Runner was ready . . .

PENNY DEAN

Penny Dean is a real woman. She was born in California, America, on 21 March 1955. On 29 July 1978, Penny Dean swam from Shakespeare Beach in Dover, England, to Cap Gris-Nez in France. She took only seven hours and forty minutes to swim across the English Channel! Penny Dean is the fastest Channel swimmer of all time.

EXERCISES

Vocabulary Work

Look back at the 'Dictionary Words' in this story. Make sure that you know the meaning of each word.

1 Look at the pictures and answer the questions with the right words.

Look at the picture on page 12

a What are the people in this picture doing?

b What is the right word for this group of people?

c What is the right name for the man who is standing up?

Look at the picture on page 20

a What is the right word for the animal eating the banana?

b The animal is sitting on . . . What?

c Where are all these people?

2 Write sentences with the words in these groups.

a science/facts/life

b members/committee/support/chairman/meeting

c beat (verb)/trials/track

d boycott/race (noun)/stadium/protest (noun)

e chimpanzee/zoo

f crazy/flat (adjective)

Comprehension

Chapters 1–4

1 Who in these chapters . . .

a . . . thought he was the school's best ten thousand metres runner?

b . . . gave Mary a book about Penny Dean?

c . . . got thirty-six questions about North Africa right?

d . . . said that he supported Mary's ideas?

Chapters 5–8

2 Put the two parts of the sentences together.

a James didn't know the mystery runner because . . .
b Mark Hudson wasn't with the runners because . . .
c Mary dressed like a chimpanzee because . . .
d Mr Drummond was angry with Mary because . . .

. . . she thought people would notice her.
. . . she was dressed like a chimpanzee.
. . . she wore a hat.
. . . he hurt his foot.

Chapters 9–12

3 Who in these chapters said . . .?

a 'Are you trying to be funny, Curtis?'

b 'They *can* stop me from running if they want to.'

c 'And who *doesn't* want me to put Mary Maloney's name on the list?'

d 'So how was the meeting?'

Chapters 13–16

4 Finish these sentences:

a Mary kissed Peter because . . .

b Mrs Drummond told her husband that . . .

c The race the reporters and TV people were interested in was . . .

Discussion

1 Do you think men are better than women? Why/why not? What can a man do better than a woman? What can a woman do better than a man?

2 Do you think all scientific facts are true? Why/why not?

3 Penny Dean was Mary's hero. Who is *your* hero? Is it a sportswoman? Someone on TV? Someone in your family?

Writing

1 Write about your hero (150 words). Why is he or she your hero? Has he or she changed your life?

2 On page 23 Peter Morris telephones James Curtis. We only have Peter's half of the conversation. Write James' part of the conversation.